BANGKOK
THAT WAS

FABRIZIO LA TORRE

BANGKOK
THAT WAS

*Photographs
1956 – 1961*

Edited by François Bayle

Serindia Publications, Chicago
& Brussels Art Edition, Belgium

Bangkok That Was is made possible with the generous support of :

ITALIAN EMBASSY - BANGKOK

BELGIAN EMBASSY - BANGKOK

 **European Parliament.** DASE Delegation for relations with the countries of Southeast Asia and the Association of Southeast Asian Nations (ASEAN).

Thai Airways International
Founded 1960

First flight to Hong Kong, 1960

First Flight to Tokyo, Japan, 1960

First flight to Kathmandu, Nepal, 1968

First flight to Rome, Italy, 1974

Fabrizio La Torre

Preface

It was before I was born when Fabrizio La Torre came to live in Bangkok from 1956 to 1961, and took these photos which were very typical of his style, humane, sensitive and warm. Wherever he was, in Rome, the city of his birth, in North America, in New York and in Canada during a six-month trip, or during those five years spent in Thailand and Asia, as a photographer he never abandoned his personal and caring view of the people, the moments of whose daily lives he was consigning to film.

It was before I was born, and yet, when I looked at these photos I felt I could recognise the city and the way of life which our parents talked to us about, made up of spontaneity, true feelings and, at the same time, a strong desire to modernise our capital without sacrificing its soul.

Fabrizio was not content to be one of those photographers who were just passing through, producing a quick photo report for a travel magazine, and that was why his photos expressed things which were beautiful and true about our recent past. He wanted to know and understand Thailand through the experiences and the acquaintances which made a mark on him.

As a member of the small team which launched the company Italthai Industrial, he was familiar with life on the Chao Phraya, viewed not simply from the riverbank but also by standing on the hefty barge which was dredging it. As an art enthusiast, he soon befriended Silpa Bhirasri (Corrado Feroci) and collaborated with him in photographing ancient lacquer cabinets conserved in the National Museum Bangkok. Towards the end of World War II, when he was involved in the fighting as part of the Allied Secret Service, he met Jim Thompson, who was older than him, also an art enthusiast and formerly an eminent secret agent. He was quick to form relationships with all, thanks to his great curiosity and his desire to become better acquainted with our country and its culture.

It is an honour and a pleasure to reveal to you these magnificent photos, the work of probably the most Thai of Italian photographers.

Shane Suvikapakornkul
Serindia Publications

Fabrizio La Torre,
An Italian-Thai History

The scene took place in November 2008 in Bordighera, a small, pretty seaside town on the Italian Riviera, to which my uncle, Fabrizio La Torre, my mother's brother, had decided to retire and end his days. But the autumn weather was horrible; uninterrupted rain and cold winds had transformed this town which was pleasant and joyful under the summer sun into an awful, grey setting, bereft of holidaymakers.

Fabrizio was living alone, he never married, had no children and, apart from his nephews, did not see anyone very much, because, as he admitted with obvious sadness, all his friends had, one after another, departed this life.

There we were, huddled together in this tiny flat which he had sparsely furnished with the bare necessities, as if he wished to rid himself of the superfluous things which so often clutter our lives, and as the weather forecast was promising heavy rain for several days, I was racking my brains for something to fill the long grey hours ahead of us.

I remembered something my mother and my grandmother used to tell me, that Fabrizio, in a much earlier period of his life, had been a marvellous photographer. Photos! What a good idea. I questioned him: whatever became of those photos, and could I see them? From his replies I gathered that he set no great story by these remnants of a very distant past, but he too had observed the awful weather, so he agreed. From the bottom of cupboards and even the cellar, there rapidly emerged a mass of boxes, packages and files, quickly amounting to a cubic metre in volume!

I dived in and didn't resurface for several hours, captivated by what I discovered: a body of work by an artist with a structure, well thought out, consistent, thoroughly imbued with that Italian Neo-realism of the 1950–1960s, so familiar to us from the cinema but pervaded by a strongly humanistic approach revealing to us human beings doing the same things, toiling at the same tasks, experiencing the same joys and fears regardless of whether they were Italians, Europeans, Americans, Thais or Japanese. He chose a

Fabrizio as a young officer cadet at the Italian Naval Academy in 1941 on the gangway of a training ship.

One of the vessels used by the newly created company Italthai Industrial for the dredging of the river Chao Phraya in Bangkok.

forthright universalist approach, completely at odds with the nationalisms of the 1940s and the wars they brought about. An artist's response to the horrors of the conflicts still so fresh in our memories.

It went without saying that the remaining time spent in Bordighera with Fabrizio flew by, the execrable weather for the season was immediately forgotten and I hardly raised my eyes from this extraordinary treasure. Those cloud-laden days were the starting point of an extraordinary adventure, beginning with the process of restoration and digitisation of the photos under the watchful eye of the artist himself, and continuing with the organisation of exhibitions in France, Belgium and Italy and finally Bangkok, in art galleries, prestigious venues and museums. During these first few years when the artist was still with us and could assist us, we could prevail upon him to search his memory, to tell us about this or that trip, the people he met and the professionals he befriended and the anecdotes which brought to life his works.

Fabrizio left us in the summer of 2014 but right to the very end he wrote his texts by hand or typed them on an old Remington typewriter, as well as dictating and recording commentaries to help us to understand better his photographic work and his life, which sometimes resembled a novel.

He was born in 1921 Rome, but spent the first years of his life in Northern Italy, first in Milan and then in that "villa" (the Italian word used to describe what elsewhere might have been called a chateau or a palace) with its 75 rooms, its private chapel, ballroom and salons decorated with frescoes painted by a very great artist of the 18th century.

In his family, everyone seemed to possess and artistic talent, without making a fuss about or impose it on others. Discretion and modesty reign: his father, a brilliant cavalry officer, spoke six languages fluently, painted and sculpted, published pastiches of Molière and Proust as well as a historical work on Pope Alexander VI Borgia. His mother, Gabriella, regaled her friends with a flood of sublime porcelain and ended her life as a stylist for Maison Hermès. As for his sister, she first raised her four children

In the 1860s Fabrizio's grandfather, Enrico Valenziani, a passionate photographer and one of the first Italian practitioners of the art, took some remarkable shots of the city of Rome, such as this view of Saint Peter's Square on Easter Sunday 1863 on the occasion of the Papal Blessing.

Fabrizio, age 3, with his mother Gabriella and his sister Nicoletta in 1924 in Cannes on the French Riviera.

before embarking on producing sculptures made of coral and seashells, which would be found on sale in the boutiques of Pierre Cardin. But none of them would claim to be an artist.

As an adolescent, Fabrizio chose a form of artistic expression which he thought was exclusively his own: photography.

Several important dates stood out in the life of this photographer. First 1941, when, after a first year at university, he joined the Naval Academy in Livorno and became an officer cadet in the navy. War was on and for the first time he left the shelter of family life; it was his first experience as an adult: he applied for, and, very exceptionally, received permission to take his camera on board. He was demobilised in December 1945, having taken part in the liberation of Venice.

Then, from December 1946 until August 1948, he was in South America, to which he travelled in search of employment, if possible in the merchant navy, and from which he returned no richer than before but with his eyes full of the marvels hidden in distant lands. Being too impecunious to give full rein to his passion for photography, he swore that he would never travel so far again without a good camera and the requisite rolls of film.

His opportunity for a long trip did not come again until September 1955: for several months he travelled the length and breadth of the USA and Canada, from New York to California, from the snowy wastes of the Far North to the banks of the Saint Lawrence. And this time the camera had not been forgotten, and it captured the thousand details which make up this "New World".

Starting in August 1956, and lasting until March 1961, his "great adventure", so longed-for, finally happened: he got a job in a public works company which had been commissioned by the World Bank to dredge and clean the Chao Phraya, the great river which flows through Bangkok. For him it was a five-year long opportunity to discover

Commander Crabb, British underwater warfare specialist, whose adventures inspired the character of James Bond and with whom Fabrizio worked at the end of the war.

Italthai Industrial diver during operations to refloat wrecks in Bangkok's waters.

At the end of World War II, Crabb commanded a group of combat divers in Italy, of which Fabrizio was one.

Thailand and part of Asia at a time when mass tourism did not yet exist.

As he said himself, this stay made a profound impression on him, giving him a serenity, a sense of balance which rapidly translated into an acuteness of vision. When he returned to Rome, marked by his Asian experience, he was able to capture the everyday life of his contemporaries with remarkable humanity and affection.

At the end of the 1960s, two unexpected events affected the life of Fabrizio. First, success came knocking. His photos had been noticed, gallery owners and publishers offered to exhibit and publish his photographs. Should he have acknowledged himself as an artist? It was out of the question... And then there was the discovery of the works of Enrico Valenziani, his grandfather, to whom the Italian state and the City of Rome decided to pay tribute. He was a photographer! He was actually one of the "fathers" of Italian photography. Today the Valenziani fund is owned by the Italian state and is regularly exhibited. Is that the reason? Or is it something more obscure? From that point on Fabrizio stopped all photographic activity, gave away or sells his cameras, closed his archives and put them away in crates where they will remain hidden for 40 years!

In 2009 he agreed to allow his archives to be re-opened and studied, that some negatives be restored and that, gradually, a first exhibition on Rome in the years 1950-1960 be organised using them. Presented at the Italian Cultural Institute in Paris, the exhibition was a major success. The events came thick and fast after that: in Belgium, the FNAC in Brussels and in Liège host exhibitions of his photos, and most notably, the Modern Art Museum of Ixelles (Brussels) repeated and added to the exhibition on Rome.

At this point the artist was 90 years old and his health was worsening. He realised that this was no time to hesitate and decided to contribute fully to the restoration of his works. He moved to Brussels where he had the benefit of the experts and technicians which he would need. It was the start of a race against the clock, against illness and death. The photos were inventoried, restored, printed in accordance with the detailed instructions of La Torre. Right to the very end, his mind was lucid enough to come up

Fabrizio La Torre's simple but welcoming house where he liked to receive his friends when they passed through Bangkok and to show them the beauties of this country.

with a mass of information indispensable for a full understanding of his work.

In September 2014, thanks to the patronage and active support of HSH Prince Albert II of Monaco, the first Retrospective of his works opened in the Principality in an exhibition covering 800 square metres, displaying 250 photos, representing all the geographical areas covered by this travelling photographer, Italy, North America and Asia. A catalogue was published to mark the event.

For a whole year, Fabrizio helped daily with preparations for this Retrospective. He made decisions on the tiniest details. He knew this was his last chance to show his work exactly as he wished it to be seen. Alas, two weeks before the official inauguration, his heart gave out. His ashes would be placed in the little cemetery next to the Principality, in Cap d'Ail where his parents and his sister were already at rest.

The exhibition organised in Bangkok at the end of 2018 is an opportunity to plunge even more deeply into these archives and make some surprising discoveries, such as these few minutes of 16mm film which so fully confirm our understanding of his art. These photos are not an exercise in nostalgia, they are encounters between the unexpected and the eternal, a mixture which this photographer poet was able to capture and show to us.

I have the great honour of being the person who brought together the skills and the desires of all those involved so that you can discover Fabrizio La Torre. My thanks to all who made this undertaking possible.

François Bayle
Curator, Exhibition Commissioner
Executor of Fabrizio La Torre's will

LOOK ❖ *Guardare*

Guardare – to look at.

"I have no objection to landscape photographs. I realise I didn't take many. And when I did I nearly always introduced some human elements.

When it was possible... Sometimes a monument in a city – the Eiffel Tower in Paris, Saint Peter's Square in Rome, the Grand Palace in Bangkok – or a very specific landscape grab our attention because they are there, right in the middle of everything and denying their presence and visual impact would be pointless.

But as far as possible I always kept my distance from the "wonders of this world". It all began in my youth. My parents gave me my first camera, a Bakelite body with non-adjustable lens and focus which produced rather strange half format 18x24 millimetre negatives. That's how I started taking photos.

I proudly showed them to my parents who thought they were "very pretty". That was when my mother said, "they look just like postcards". Her tone of voice revealed to me what she, a real artist herself, felt about my first photos... I was only a child then, but I immediately understood the mistake I must never repeat: just trying to capture what was pretty.

Take the example of a marvellous sunset: what could be more beautiful? When is the best time to photograph it? When you can catch the balance between the light and the dark? The celebrated "sfumature"? Not really! You always end up trapped in what I call "postcardism" which my mother, despite her maternal feelings for me, had so cruelly identified in my first photos.

In passing, I thought I had invented the term "postcardism" to describe what I hated but a young friend of mine who was literature-inclined recently pointed out this quote from Jean Cocteau talking about Picasso: "Picasso taught me to outrun beauty. Let me explain: if you only run as fast as beauty you can only produce pleonasms and postcardism. If you run less fast than beauty the result can only be mediocrity. If you can run faster than beauty, your work will seem ugly but it will force beauty to catch up and once it catches you it will become true beauty."

In photography I had understood something: only by introducing the human element which is spontaneous, unpredictable, with an obvious story or a hidden one, can we avoid postcardism.

That's why I so rarely photograph a bare landscape.

In any case, "bare" landscapes are becoming a rarity, because man has left his footprint virtually everywhere on this planet. I well remember a series of photos I took in Bangkok on the Chao Phraya of the enormous machine which we used to dredge the river bottom. Not a human being in sight, just a massive tangle of metal beams, chains, black and greasy gears. A monster. Above the main arch which supported the lifting system was written its name in giant letters "ARCHIMEDE" as if the machine were shouting his name at us. It was almost anthropomorphic."

It is not easy to recognise the Thai capital in this expanse of little houses as far as the eye can see, the horizon clearly visible, and flat, not a skyscraper in sight, no "condos". *Bangkok that was!*

La Torre was not a fan of landscape photography. It was always the human dimension which interested him. Nonetheless, this cart drawn by an emaciated ox on a beach at low tide looks like the beginning of a story with man as its principal actor.

Wat Arun, before the banks of the river in front of the temple were developed.

The same river which majestically irrigates the buildings of the temples and palaces also brings to the city of Bangkok everything it needs to build and feed itself.

Having been brought from the northern provinces following the natural course of the rivers, these bundles of bamboo arrive in Bangkok for use on building sites.

The Mahakarn Fort and the Golden Mountain Temple in the background, in the sunshine but also emerging from the early morning mist, like a steamer coming into port. Anyone who is familiar with the traffic jams in Bangkok will enjoy the image of this pedicab disappearing in the emptiness, without actually believing it. You can still see the small wooden houses, which have since made way for a green area, crowded between the fort and the temple. On the corner, opposite the fort, on the right of the photo, you can see the front of the cinema shown in a photograph on page 64.

Harmony: a moment when man and nature demonstrate that they can co-exist, showing mutual respect. Though the hand of man is present everywhere in this image of this fisherman's hut and his nets spread out to dry, its beauty also lies in the distant silhouette of this temple fitting perfectly into the vegetation.

Even in the 1950s, Fabrizio was amused and sometimes irritated by the words which invaded the countryside to promote a product or declare the pride of a company. Two photos taken on the Chao Phraya, the enormous re-flotation barge belonging to Italthai Industrial which seems to shout out its name "ARCHIMEDE" in enormous letters so that no-one forgets, and the petrol station whose famous Shell emblem seems entirely appropriate in the marine context.

RESPECT ❖ *Rispettare*

Rispettare — to respect.

"Respect is an integral part of photography. At least in my case. Respect begins with the subjects. Of course the photographer is appropriating a moment of their private lives, of their truth but if the relationship is going to work you must never try to show them in an negative light nor in an aggressive, embarrassing nor shameful one.

An element of humour in a picture is perfectly acceptable and the subjects are the first to realise this and accept it. In my Rome photos, for example, I can remember a number of shots of religious subjects, a cardinal, a group of nuns, whose demeanour, for a brief moment, might have caused a smile. I seized that moment without a trace of criticism or malice. Those photos, even today, are poetic and beautiful. Because they are true.

During the years when I was taking those photos, to stroll through the city with a camera dangling on your shoulder, was viewed with good-humoured indifference. People were amused to allow themselves to be photographed. Afterwards, the paparazzi came along, the news magazine photographers, the age of the hard-hitting image, raw, frequently violent and then the camera lens came to be regarded with open suspicion, even with hostility.

It became impossible to take the kind of photo which I liked to take, ones which showed the simple truth of a human being, in all sincerity.

The doctor's house. This belonged to the medical practitioner who cared for the Italian community of Bangkok. His house might not have been far from the river and was well used to the invasive high waters, since it was built on stilts to keep doctor and patients dry.

Another thing you have to learn to respect is nature! The weather, the light, the temperature, the humidity.

A few months before arriving in Thailand, I was in North America, in Canada. I had taken the brand new Canadian Pacific train to travel to Toronto and I was delighted by the light effects which the Canadian winter bestowed on me. At every stop I would get off to take a few photos, in the midst of walls of snow and gusts of icy wind. However, I hadn't realised that with temperatures of at least 20° below zero, my films would not survive for long: only a few photos could be salvaged.

In Bangkok, I learned to be careful about the humidity, the rain and also the excessive heat of the sun. And I learned to enjoy making use of what nature offered us: a river in flood which swamped half the city, a morning mist which transformed monuments into ghostly ships drifting on unknown seas.

In those days, special effects produced using electronics were unknown. The only special effects available came from the photographer's complicity with the elements of nature."

What could more perfectly illustrate respect for nature than these buffaloes and their keeper crossing a rice paddy whilst causing no more than a slight lapping of the water? Harmony.

On these hefty boats, it is not just the commercial cargo (materials or food) that the "pilot" has to bring safely to port. Usually, his whole family lives on this floating home, which gives some sense of the responsibility borne by these men and women who, with only the help of a pole, have to steer their way through strong, sometimes wild currents.

Two examples of traditional fishing methods common to Thailand and to Fabrizio's Italy; hunting tiny crabs as the tide goes out and especially trabucco fishing, waiting for the moment when, following the movement of the tides, the shoals of fish always follow the same route in order to reach the areas rich in food. Trabucco fishing has always attracted artists, painters and photographers because of the picturesque nature of its equipment; nowadays, however, in Europe and in Asia, dwindling resources and water pollution have led to the disappearance of most of these nets.

The talent of the photographer: giving life to a scene where nothing
is happening. Conveying the idea of movement where everything
is still. You have to track the movement of one of these boats, see
it coming from afar, prepare for the framing of the shot which will
make it the centre of attention when it is actually only a minor part.
It provides the scale for the hay stack, for the bamboo hut, for the
vegetation. It is reassuring too, because it shows the possibility of
a human presence in such harmonious peaceful landscapes, which
are so sublime on occasion that some might fear not being accepted.
That is the talent of the photographer, but of a photographer who
has been profoundly imbued with the philosophical values which he
discovered in Thailand.

Two faces of the same city: the tumultuous waters where this man, with the build of an athlete, steers his boat using his strength, and those of the never-ending floods which invade gardens and homes, showing why so many buildings are on stilts.

In the potters' district, the high-water does not trouble the artisans whose enormous vases are too heavy to be swept away. It doesn't stop the children playing either, nor their amusement on seeing the photographer paddling in the water looking for the right angle for the shot.

LIVE ❖ *Vivere*

Vivere — to live.

"Everyday life... Everyday life. Yes, that is what has always interested me the most. But for a very simple reason: going from one country to another, from one culture to another, everything seems so different and yet...everything is very much the same! Even the symbols, the "totems" are identical. Did Gustave Eiffel ever imagine that one day, from Tokyo to Las Vegas by way of China, people would build replicas of his tower?

If you observe everyday life, you will see how universal human nature is. Despite what racists and extremists may think, we really are all the same, we all aspire to a better life for ourselves and those close to us, we try to keep illness, old age and death at bay, we gaze at the sky and try to understand the meaning of life.

My photos were taken during the period 1950-1960. As I told you, back in those days you could still photograph people in the street. Afterwards, they became almost hostile when faced by a camera. Now things are worse. We are no longer "people", human beings. We've become models, actors playing roles in artificial, fictional lives.

Now, because of society's obsession with "image", when every smartphone contains an excellent camera, we've all become producers, ferociously protective of our own images, not allowing anyone else to photograph us, whilst at the same time, bombarding our friends with images of our daily lives.

Lives in which everyone has an idiotic smile, pretending to be perfectly happy. It's still everyday life perhaps, but it no longer has the same vitality, the same truth as what I was lucky enough to be able to capture.

In Thailand, for example, I took several photos of mothers looking after their young children. I would like to tell you what struck me in the case of these women.

I come from a country, Italy, and a continent, Europe, which were devastated by the horrors of war. At the time I was myself a young naval officer in the years 1941–1942, and when I was ashore I saw the violence, the fighting, the bombing, the hunger suffered by the civilian population. I saw incredibly strong and brave women demonstrating unbelievable energy to protect and feed their children so as to give them a chance to live and grow.

And it was precisely that which I experienced in Bangkok and in the countryside when I photographed their daily lives, the lives of these dauntless, loving Thai mothers! Thanks to them, whatever the family background, I could see that these kids were off to a good start.

Some specialists in the art of photography have said wonderful things about so-called "everyday life photos" but in all honesty, I have to admit I classify under that heading mostly snapshots. A question of luck. I've never considered myself to be a good portrait photographer. I don't think I can produce a good portrait to order. Except perhaps with children, but that is because they can't hide their true feelings. If I have occasionally managed to capture a few seconds of truth, believe me, it was pure luck. Nothing more."

Private or public transport, on water and dry land, the two systems co-exist.

When His Majesty King Bhumibol Adulyadej (Rama IX r.1946–2016) crossed Bangkok, his people waited for a very long time to catch a glimpse of their King. In the image on the opposite page (top), you could see some people sheltering from the sun, along the shadow of a streetlight, whilst others, better prepared, had brought their umbrellas, but all pressed close when they saw the Rolls Royce of the King. And then, as all traffic came to a halt to see the King go by, his faithful subjects created a guard of honour for him which modern security precautions would never allow today.

It is a paradox which has struck many travellers who have come to visit the Kingdom of Siam over the centuries: the Thais are not what you would call a seafaring race, confronting the oceans of the globe, their storms and their endlessness, and yet, in reality, they spend a large part of their lives on water, the water of immense raging rivers whose currents are sometimes deadly, on which they demonstrate a remarkable facility. The art of having sea legs when one is actually sedentary is one startling feature of a people who are doubtless too happy at home to launch themselves into the dangers of a seafaring adventure.

Facing the powerful ever-flowing waters of the Chao Phraya, these two young people seem to be telling each other secrets without fear that the river of life will carry them far away. They are in their own world and nothing can disturb them.

Can we spot the many human beings who seem to be hiding in this incredible tangle of boats and pots?

Does it take courage or foolhardiness to bathe or wash in the murky waters of the river and its klongs (canals)? Everything or nearly everything used to arrive in Bangkok by river, and rather too many things returned to it – waste water, rubbish – given the lack of sanitary disposal systems and purification plants.

Two examples of street food in Bangkok, a mother and her five
children playing in the "shop" and a Chinese cook amused by the
interest shown by the gastronomically inclined photographer.

Appearances can be deceptive: observing the choice place which is given to them, the particular care shown to them, you might think that children in Thailand have always enjoyed the status which their peers in Western countries have recently attained, that of "little emperors" who can do what they like, who are the centre of attention for adults. It is not actually the case. It is not the child who is mistakenly fetishised but rather the family, this core unit, which takes on many forms, where the attention lavished on children is only equalled by the respect shown to the elderly, where exchanges between generations bind people together, where anyone can receive help and be comforted, whatever the problem, trouble at work or a broken heart.

This all comes to mind quite naturally when looking at this mother carrying and holding her two kids or these adolescents who are quite happy to talk with the elderly and enjoy the benefit of their experience.

Bangkok trams are the "modern elephants" transporting people
and packages with a clanging noise which warns everyone of their
approach.

Street scene in Chinatown. Tiny stalls, street hawkers, pedal-driven *tuk tuk*, the technology, the machines may have changed but the atmosphere remains the same.

Though on a world-wide scale, the fame of Thai cinema is rather put in the shade by the flashy Indian productions of Bollywood, Thailand remains nonetheless the first Asian country to give pride of place to this art form. Starting in the 1920s, the local cinema industry begins making original productions, such as the documentary entitled Sam Poi Luang: Great Celebration in the North, produced with the Royal Railway Company to advertise rail travel. The first work of fiction is produced in 1927, the first "talkie" in 1932 only five years after the first American talking picture and three years after the first French one, two countries with the leading film industries of the time.

Having for a long time been considered a technically evolved form of puppet theatre, Thai cinema retained a festive air with a taste for the spectacular over a long period, calling for gaudy, multicoloured decorations on the front of cinemas.

WORK ❖ *Lavorare*

Lavorare — to work.

"Man is never more interesting than when talking about his work, about his calling. And he is frequently happy to display his work, his actions, his techniques. Whether he is a surgeon, a cabinetmaker, a fisherman or a cook, he is rightly proud of what he does. For a photographer it is an opportunity too good to be missed.

When I arrived in Thailand in August 1956, I knew nothing about that country in particular nor Asia in general. I had been taken on as an office manager in a newly created business by the name of "Italthai Industrial", set up by Giorgio Berlingieri, an engineer from Genoa. The company had been awarded a contract by the World Bank for the dredging of the Chao Phraya river and the removal of the wrecks of the old cargo ships which were hampering the river traffic. Though my job was actually land-based, in an office, I freely admit that whenever I boarded the dredger or one of our other vessels, I never forgot to take my Exacta, my trusty camera, always on the lookout for two or three interesting shots.

There was a diver whose size and girth fascinated me. When he was underwater, like a weightless astronaut, he acquired an agility which was denied him by gravity when he returned to the surface...

Back in those days, Thailand had not yet acquired the industrial muscle it has now. Most people worked in farming or as artisans and it was these "street" trades which made life and the city so much more enjoyable, because you could always find good, simple food for a modest price to fill your stomach or a cobbler to sole your shoes or a man on a Vespa more than willing to cross the city and its traffic jams to deliver an urgent package.

But even then, throughout the country, you could feel the desire to learn about industrial techniques, to learn and to become "modern" without delay. I remember Italthai came up with the idea of organising what was rather pompously called a "Trade Fair" which was basically a corrugated iron hanger open on all sides in which we presented the products of a number of Italian companies, ranging from breeze blocks to mopeds and, in particular, three wheelers, motor vehicles which you steered like a scooter but which had quite a large isothermal compartment at the back in which you could transport fresh food without it being spoiled by the heat. They sold like hot cookies!

Though I was only there to take photos, I found myself in the middle of a lively discussion with a group of young people, students who wanted to become engineers, chemists or architects who were passionately interested in the techniques on show. In the light of the technical progress achieved both in Europe and Asia, what was on show at this "fair" was almost prehistoric.

My personal preferences drew me more towards arts and crafts, an area in which a mixture of technical expertise, sureness of touch, ancestral knowledge and individual creativity caught my eye. In Thailand as in numerous Asian countries, even bearing in mind the specific character of each one, I confess to having been often carried away, enthralled by what I was lucky enough to see. I came away with a burning desire to work with my hands as they did. I was able to do so when I returned to Rome and I began by producing a number of woodcarvings."

On the barge run by the recently formed company Italthai Industrial for dredging the bottom of the Chao Phraya and removing the wrecks which hampered the river traffic.

At the first "trade fair" organised by Italthai Industrial, the stand displaying its work on the river and in the marine environment with the giant barge Archimede. Right-hand page: the diver and his assistants prepare the next dive.

The Memorial Bridge, inaugurated in 1932, the work of a British engineer, used to be a moveable bridge. Alas the mechanism is now outdated and has since been made immoveable. In the 1950s it was the only bridge over the Chao Phraya; to avoid traffic jams, small ferries were also in use to get from one side to the other.

Memorial Bridge and large dryers for fishing nets. The photographer amuses himself with the straight, almost hard lines of man-made constructions, metal beams or bamboo canvases, the plump curves of the transport or fishing boats and the glittering waves of the river water. Two very different places but two photos which communicate with each other.

Women fishing with nets, probably north of Bangkok. Fabrizio La Torre's photos illustrate the way in which Thai women were active everywhere in all aspects of the their country's economy, farm work included.

It is quite hard to glimpse this little girl weaving along the gunwale of her boat, amongst the vases and pots. In his notes the artist writes, *"Children of Thailand, children of water, nurtured, raised on these houseboats, small river junks; these children spent more time on water than on land. It was not unusual to see five- or six-year old children rowing and steering boats in the throng of the canals and the floating market."* And on the subject of this pastry seller he adds: *"I admired the skill of these women, paddling not just to move forward on their boats but above all to keep their balance and prevent their pile of sweet pastries, so neatly stored, from ending up in the water."*

The water carrier. Righ-hand page: The indefatigable drivers of "pedicabs" near the Memorial Bridge. Two "little" jobs, mostly based on muscular strength, in this period of economic recovery, which gave work to anyone who needed it. The motorised *tuk tuk*, the modernisation of the city, and above all the growth of employment in service industries have meant it is now possible to earn a living in jobs which are not as hard or exhausting.

The joys of street food, pan-fried doughs and their ingredients.

A natural and healthy delicacy – pieces of freshly cut sugar cane.

Having been created to tender for a contract of the World Bank for the purpose of rehabilitating the river and the port of Bangkok, the Italthai Industrial company also had the idea of organising a trade fair in order to bring together Italian and Thai businesses. These were the simple and rather endearing beginnings of what became a worldwide enterprise.

Thailand like Europe was discovering the convenience of "modern" household appliances.

In a corrugated iron hanger, also for sale, the first exhibitors meet their customers.

BREATH ❖ *Respirare*

Respirare — to breathe.

"There is a question I have been asked frequently, I suppose because it is an obvious one. Is there a difference in my photos, for example those taken in Rome, before and after my stay in Thailand? What it boils down to is: did my stay in Asia change the way I saw the world, people, life?

How could it be otherwise? But we still have to agree on what these Asian societies were able to give to me. It is frequently said, for example, that Buddhist countries have a different attitude to time compared to us Europeans, Westerners, who are thought to be always in a hurry, always frantic. In my case, this rather "zen" view of time flowing did not change anything very much, since I was born in Rome, a city more than 2,000 years old, where vestiges of the past are all around you, where you are reminded of eternity on every street corner. A Roman knows there is always a good reason for taking it slow.

The harmony between human beings and their planet, this Earth bestowed on man so that he could "live and prosper in peace"? As far as I know, all religions, absolutely all, have a dimension which today we would call "ecological", the concept of the garden of Eden where man and nature live in happy, peaceful equilibrium. When you see that, whatever the dominant religion in any given region, the whole of our planet is assailed by pollution, the plundering of flora and fauna, the destruction of the environment, you realise that, in this respect at least, no religion can claim moral superiority over any other.

An almost philosophical result of my stay in Thailand is definitely moderation, the refusal to accumulate superfluous goods, to possess a mass of things of which we become prisoners. Immediately after the war and the privations it brought with it, I got into the habit of living unencumbered, travelling light, of having few needs notwithstanding the temptations of the emergent consumer society. And after five years in Bangkok I was convinced of the need to refuse accumulation. And I have remained faithful to this my whole life.

You may think that these vaguely spiritual considerations are getting us off the subject of photography. But not at all! In photography, too, my experience has been that a successful photo never materialises from the accumulation of equipment, lenses and filters. You are just weighing yourself down for no reason, and all this clutter slows you down and deprives you of the reactivity and spontaneity which are indispensable.

If only you could have seen the camera I used mostly, an Exakta, made in Dresden in 1947 or 1948, with pre-war components, which I bought in Germany in 1953 when I was there on a visit to see my sister and her husband who was a diplomat in Bonn. Even I find it hard to believe that you could take quality photos with such a "thing": heavy and hard to handle; despite everything it was my trusty and sturdy camera with which I worked all over the world for all those years.

For me, a photographer is like a singer who has to have the lung capacity, the respiration to perform, not needing to use any complicated techniques. Breathe! Draw air into your lungs and into your photos, give life a chance to attach itself to your film. Take the time to understand the real harmony of what is all around you."

Two faces of the same river, Archimede with its tons of
steel finally takes a rest and the river vendor's small boat
overloaded with household goods.

When the huge barge stops work, when the hellish
grinding of pulleys and steel cables disappears, it is time
to enjoy the beauty of the scene, like a sea view balcony.

Bangkok, frequently referred to as "Venice of the East", viewing it through the lens of his camera, Fabrizio La Torre had fun with the similarities to the "City of the Doges", the span of a bridge, looking so like the "Bridge of Sighs", the prow of these boats which, if they curved back a little further, would rival those of their cousins, the gondolas.

Traffic jam: no harm done as long as no-one has to move their boat!

This photo, which is striking for its graphic impact as well as touching in its lyricism, was chosen by his Highness Prince Albert II of Monaco for inclusion in the Grimaldi Photographic Collection, one of the most remarkable in the world, to showcase the talent of this artist, following his visit to the La Torre Retrospective in Monaco.

Feast days in the temples. From Fabrizio's notes: *"How many temples are there in Bangkok? How many thousands of statues of the Buddha? In nearly five years spent over there I was never able to answer these questions. There were too many! I liked to go to these tranquil spots, protected from the city by the outer walls, surrounded by perfectly maintained parks, where I often found myself alone listening to the birdsong and inhaling the perfume of the flowers. However, when the days of the religious festivals came round, these oases of peace were transformed into swarming, noisy concentrations of people where countless numbers, bearing colourful offerings, pressed at the feet of the statues."*

Fabrizio never talked much about his sentimental attachments, though he was fond of this photo with its natural harmony, notwithstanding the extreme austerity of the scene. According to him, "it was all about the little splash of white in the smile."

Who was she? Fabrizio recalled that she was English, that she was seated against this pile of wood, no doubt a pyre prepared for some ritual or other, and that as she gazed into the distance, she seemed absent, aloof from the present moment. And that junk at anchor, despite having its sails unfurled, simply added to the strangeness of the scene. That was all it took for the photographer to come up with a shot which is almost a surreal painting.

PROTECT ❖ *Proteggere*

Proteggere — to protect.

"I never had children. I never married. It just didn't happen, though my stay in Bangkok nearly brought me a wife I could love. But when the opportunity presented itself, I was not very well established in my job. My future was uncertain. In those days, when a man got married, he was supposed to be able to offer his wife and children a certain level of material comfort, which I couldn't.

Afterwards, when I obtained a job in Rome working for a Japanese airline, a job I held until my retirement — how can I put this? — the question no longer arose. I had other family obligations incumbent upon me.

The 20th century, the one I experienced, has been horrific in many ways, but particularly so in one respect: for the first time in human history children were deliberately and methodically targeted. World War II, the horrors of the Nazis, then the so-called "regional" conflicts, Korea, Vietnam, Laos, Cambodia, the Middle East and more. Everywhere there was a deliberate attempt to kill the children so that future generations would not rise up not just to seek revenge but also to seek justice.

The barbaric concept of "ethnic cleansing" requires the massacre of children by the use of weapons, organised genocide but also by forced displacement and by starvation. Letting children starve, is there any more depraved crime?

Throughout my life, I have always tried to donate from the little I had to support those organisations, NGOs like UNICEF and many others that fight to help children.

However, there are other ways of protecting children. Fortunately! It means doing everything possible to preserve in them the "magic" of childhood, that special moment in life when the little human being has not yet been weighed down by social niceties, adult ambitions, the moment when he dreams of his future life, decides what he wants to be "when he grows up".

I have been fortunate enough always to get on well with children, perhaps because I employed to photograph them the same techniques I used with adults, being discreet, unobtrusive, quiet without disturbing their games. They would end up forgetting I was there.

One photograph I took in Thailand is a particular favourite of mine; it is of a little girl of six or seven years of age, no more, viewed from behind, balancing her little brother on her hip, a baby less than a year old, her body twists a little because the baby is a good size and weight! I have always viewed that scene as a demonstration of the solidarity which can be displayed by very young children, a relationship still innocent of ulterior motives or jealousy. A magical moment of childhood."

"I was trying to take a photo of the one in the middle, unsmiling. However, by the time I had got the focus right, he had called over all his pals and I ended up with this happy bunch of laughing kids. But he stayed concentrated and impassive."

You are never too young to start helping your father by rowing at
the bow of the boat.

And you are never too young to be proud of your daddy, a fisherman,
when he brings home a fish like this one.

"Cheeky!" Or mocking? The expression of this little girl reveals the taunting attitude of a child who has just played a trick or done something silly, but there is also this glance toward an adult, unimpressed by the supposed seriousness of "grown-ups". Fabrizio had great fun: in the days when he was taking these photos, people were not used to seeing cameras and frequently found them amusing, and gently made fun of the person using them; a kind of complicity between people who didn't take themselves too seriously.

Flowers as offerings, to be taken to the temple.

Arrogant! That was the photographer's description of the amusing attitude of this stark-naked little boy, protruding stomach, hands on hips, scrutinising his sister and the buffalo like a self-important potentate, master of the world. Though the photo as a whole is redolent of the sweetness of a harmonious bucolic scene, the stance of the little chap adds something unexpected, a human sentiment, grandiloquent, incongruous and funny.

TRAVEL DIARY

HMONG TRIBES
(NORTH OF THAILAND)

Nothing prepared Fabrizio La Torre for a trip to the far north of Thailand, to an area into which at the time foreigners were not really advised to venture, where tribal independence was considerable, no doubt justified by the relatively abundant cultivation of opium poppies.

But one of his friends, a diplomat at the Italian embassy in Bangkok had talked him into doing him a big favour: the embassy driver had fallen ill and there was no one to replace him on such a long trip over roads which were not always of the best quality, since only one third of the 700 kilometres to be covered was actually tarmacked. Nonetheless, Fabrizio had accepted enthusiastically, since his own escapades had been limited to Chiang Rai and Chiang Mai and no further.

They had made the trip in two days, had stopped in a little village, at the agreed spot, to wait for the guide who was to take them to the village. Another foreigner joined them, a Spanish missionary who had lived for twenty years in China and spoke the dialect of these tribes. Then, they had travelled a considerable distance before abandoning their car and completing the journey with a climb of several hours on tiny paths lost in the vegetation. Though the Hmong were nomadic, they were perfectly capable of building large, spacious huts of bamboo and thatch, which they easily dismantled when the time came to change camp.

In order to welcome the foreign diplomate and his companion, the head of the village had consulted the shaman who had passed the question on to the spirits. The latter seemed perfectly happy. The atmosphere was joyful, festive and friendly, which encouraged Fabrizio to bring out his camera and start taking a few photos.

And whilst the diplomat and the missionary were talking to the chief, the photographer was able to mingle with the daily life of the tribe, weaving, cooking, caring for the animals, and he was much taken with the beauty of the traditional costumes and the silver jewellery with which even the children were covered.

Fabrizio La Torre came and went freely in the village, and, as was his wont, exchanged smiles and signs of friendship with everyone. The group of strangers had been invited to share a meal and delicious smells were already in evidence.

However, Fabrizio could not help overhearing that the conversation between the head of the village and the diplomat seemed to be taking an unexpected turn, and becoming distinctly unfriendly shouting. He approached the group, saw that the head of the village had placed two large brown blocks like large bars of chocolate in front of him, doubtless opium paste, and he seemed to be very angry with the diplomat.

The missionary interpreter was doing his best, but tempers continued to rise. At a given moment, the diplomat signalled to the photographer to follow

him and they left the village to what sounded suspiciously like a volley of insults in the Hmong dialect. It was only at the bottom of the hill, breathless because of the speed of the descent, that the diplomat explained: the head of the village had agreed to the meeting, had prepared a feast only because he thought that the Italian was like one of his colleagues from a friendly embassy, who had been there some weeks previously to exchange opium blocks for wads of dollars... Understandably disappointed that there was no deal to be transacted, and unreceptive to the fact that the Italian Republic sent him an emissary who was admittedly friendly but not a dope fiend, the chief promptly dismissed the interlopers.

The missionary, a friend of the tribe and speaking their dialect, was the only one to be invited to the feast. And Fabrizio had the time to take some exceptional photos. He had no regrets about this long-ago escapade and he called it to mind still laughing at the misunderstanding.

HONG KONG

It is a strange twist of fate that this young Italian, fired with a burning passion to discover the world and bear witness to it through the art of photography, then finds out belatedly that his grandfather, Enrico Valenziani, was in the 1860s, one of the creators of Italian photography, which meant that he, Fabrizio, was just another "follower"!

And what about when in 1958 he finally set foot in Hong Kong, the door to China, of which he had dreamed for so long as a country, a civilisation, an art with which he had become familiar both through the beautiful works of Chinese art to be found in the houses of his family and which he had seen on a daily basis, and, above all, by the frequent mention of his great-uncle Carlo Valenziani, a larger-than-life character whom he was never able to meet but whose memory was still treasured by his family?

Carlo lived and died in Rome, (1831–1896). He was a Doctor of Philosophy and Law, and was the first professor of Chinese and Japanese at the University of Rome. As an orientalist of international renown, he published many works, including, for the first time in Europe, translations of works of Japanese fiction.

Though up to the beginning of the 1970s Fabrizio was unaware of the scope of the work of his grandfather Enrico, he was fully informed about that of his great-uncle Carlo, whose books were to be found in his parents' library. He attributed his natural affinity with Asia and his affection for the art of that region of the world to the "unsurprising" influence which Carlo exerted on his adolescent brain, thirsty for distant voyages and discoveries.

However, his discovery of China did not occur as he would have wished. Back in the 1960s, getting into the country of Mao was no easy undertaking. Afterwards, as he travelled the world on behalf of his employer, JAL, he had no time. It was only once he had retired, in the period 1990 to 2000, that he could finally discover Peking and Shanghai and return to Hong Kong, to see for himself the upheaval that had taken place in that city state. But it was not just that these countries and cities had been transformed by modernisation; above all, Fabrizio had, some time ago, given up taking artistic photos, and now he only carried around a small automatic camera which he used as a notebook.

Though Fabrizio was never one to go in for deliberate nostalgia, his Hong Kong photos instill a feeling both of nostalgia and incredulity. Is that what Aberdeen bay was like? Hard to believe! What is today just a line of skyscrapers used to have the look and charm of a small romantic bay on the Côte d'Azur. And everywhere this city, which was already bursting with a feverish, frenetic life, still seemed nonetheless to take time to cultivate its traditions in the manner that one caresses gently in one's memory the pretty images of one's childhood.

What can one say of the natural elegance of these characters from another age, he in his traditional costume, lost in thought, she, a true fashion plate, holding her oar with infinite grace, and this other figure, pensive on the edge of the quay, superb in her sheath dress, a photo to which Fabrizio gave the title "eternal feminine"?

We can talk about the inevitable evolution in this territory, rampant modernism, and it is all eminently sensible and perfectly understandable, but La Torre shows us once again and above all, through the gestures of these few persons, frozen in time, the universality of the human dimension – including the gaze of this child who appears to have been deserted by the two adults who are leaving the scene, and so focuses on the photographer whose complicity he understands.

JAPAN

In 1961, when he returned to Italy after a five-year stay in Thailand, Fabrizio La Torre intended to look after his mother, whose health was not perfect, and to attend to family matters, which had somewhat been neglected since his father's death 15 years earlier. Accordingly, he looked for a job which would allow him to be present in Rome but also let him continue the travelling habits, to which he had become so attached.

The solution was supplied by JAL, the Japanese airline which offered him first the job of communications manager and then of commercial manager for Italy, Greece and Malta. He travelled repeatedly not only to Asia but all over the world when accompanying important groups on new routes flying over the North Pole or Siberia.

At the beginning of the 1960s these trips were still unimaginably slow: turbo-prop aeroplanes could not fly any faster than 500 km/hour and had to refuel after five or six hours. Stopovers came and went, during which passengers and crew stayed overnight in the same hotel, breakfast together and then took off for the next stage of the flight, in an atmosphere akin to an Agatha Christie novel or an epic Joseph Conrad adventure.

The arrival of the jet engine gradually changed this form of travel, but it was only with the advent of the giant Boeing 747 that airline companies switched to mass transport carried out as quickly as possible and at the lowest cost. And so, in 1961, on his return from Bangkok, Fabrizio was quite proud to travel on board a Comet, first jet airliner which carried around 70 passengers at 700 km/h. Realising that this mode of travel saved him several precious days compared to earlier flights, he exploited this by following an itinerary from Bangkok to Rome by way of Calcutta, New Delhi, Istanbul and Athens. These were still the days when you really had to love travelling in order to be able to bear for so long these interminable flights.

During his career with JAL, Fabrizio flew to Asia 26 times, mostly to Japan but also to Thailand, to which he seemed to have formed an enduring attachment.

During all these trips, Fabrizio roamed around Japan in every direction by plane, of course, but also by train, car and boat. He was enthusiastic about everything, fascinated by all. His first trip there dated back to 1960. He was still living in Bangkok at the time and travelled to visit Tokyo, Osaka and Kyoto. He also particularly wanted to visit Hiroshima: it was only 15 years since the atomic bomb was dropped on that city and the aftermath is omnipresent.

A few years before his death, more than 50 years after his trip to the martyred city, he would still talk about how profoundly shaken and marked he was by what he saw in Hiroshima, by what he understood there of human folly and the boundless horrors of which our world is capable.

This profound impression, this reflection on man's destiny, this metaphysical contemplation, these were the intense emotions he admitted to trying to express after his return from his visit to Hiroshima, when he, as a photographer, viewed the *torii* of Itsukushima on the island of Miyajima. He produced a chiaroscuro photo with an almost mystical feel, heavy, in which the human element was not entirely missing but was reduced to a tiny, insignificant scale.

Japanese art was a delight to him. He rediscovered in it the materials and techniques which he had known and appreciated since his youth or his stay in Thailand: the techniques of lacquer, porcelain, prints, silk. And architecture too, the beauty of these wooden buildings (temples and houses), of these houses made of paper, whose apparent fragility defied the erosion of time. In Japan too he felt a connection, even though he admitted to having some difficulties of communication with the inhabitants, who seemed to him to be smothered by the weight of social conventions and the many rituals which burdened their working and everyday lives. Being a subtle and sensitive man, who had always made understanding others and empathy his way of life, he sometimes found the Japanese reserved to the point of coldness. However, it's not something which prevented him from loving that country nor did he only go there for his work; he went also for the pleasure of discovery which never left him.

NEPAL

For Fabrizio La Torre the road to Nepal begins in Rome! In the notes left to his nephews and nieces and in his conversations with the author, when asked about the source of this passionate interest in Asia, its inhabitants, its various cultures and art forms, Fabrizio La Torre mentioned amongst other things the fact that when he was a little boy or an adolescent, he encountered the Franco-Belgian explorer Alexandra David-Néel, who was known for having been, in 1924, the first European woman to have stayed in Lhasa, in Tibet, but who also spent almost half a century travelling in Asia.

This meant, amongst other things, that in his eyes, these encounters were not the main determining factors, but they did undeniably have an effect, given that this already extremely elderly lady made a big impression on him. She was accompanied by someone re-ferred to as "Alexandra's lama, her adopted son" whom he imagined would be young, even a child, whereas in point of fact, he turned out to be well advanced in years, and, to cap it all, this occurred without any fuss in the family home in Rome.

It was on the fourth floor of a small building, erected at the beginning of the century by his grandfather, Felice La Torre, who came from an extremely poor family of Sicilian peasants. With the help of members of the Church, he was able to go to school, pursuing his studies at the University of Medicine, and eventually becoming the leading gynaecologist in Italy, in which capacity he rose to become the Queen's personal physician and a major figure in the Italian medical world.

In this family environment, where ordinariness did not seem to be an option, the fourth floor was home to his aunt Maria, his father's sister, and her husband Percy. Maria had always been a close friend of Alexandra David-Néel, more often than not acting as typist for her manuscripts, and even offering her accommodation in Monaco, that tranquil and restful Principality, where Maria had finally chosen to settle, from April 1957.

As a child and adolescent, Fabrizio listened to the tales of madcap adventures, weeks of trekking in the Himalayas, cold, hunger, the power of meditation, but also the happiness to be felt when standing before this or that work of art.

So the idea came to him, as soon as he was able, to stop off in Kathmandu, not with the intention of finding a guide and a discreet route to get into neighbouring

Tibet, as some did, but just to savour the air, to decide if he liked these places and people, to take stock and perhaps return at a later date.

He carved out a few days in 1961 on his way back to Rome, where his family obligations await him as well as his distinctly "unsedentary" life as a manager in an airline company. You only had to look at these photos taken in Nepal to appreciate how technically accomplished he had become at capturing the moment with a camera, his cumbersome Exacta, which was not designed for it, at manipulating this harsh light which exaggerated contrasts and sculpts faces, and at blending into the scenery, into the crowd, allowing this little European to become almost invisible at a time when foreigners were still a rarity on the streets of Kathmandu.

Quite apart from the technical aspects, what was truly striking was the connection with the persons photographed, with the moments of the daily lives of a people about which he knew nothing, but, because they were human beings like him, he immediately felt a sense of closeness. Following five years spent in Thailand, getting to know the country, its beliefs, its traditions and its art, but also discovering, whenever possible, some of the major attractions of this ever-fascinating Asia, he had reached the apex of that personal philosophy which would equip him, once he returned to the city of his birth, to paint "a portrait of the Romans" which was a true work of art.

ART DIARY

Though during his lifetime, as an adolescent and during his early years as a young adult, Fabrizio La Torre endeavours to distance himself from his family surroundings, which may sometimes have seemed a little too much to bear, there is one area in which he is in complete harmony with those close to him: art, a taste for art, a natural feeling for art. From birth, art is a staple of his life; he is acquainted with its subtleties, its enticements and its subterfuges, he knows the sense of wonder it can produce and the indifference it inspires when it confines itself to an excessively academic style or tiresome repetition.

"Beautiful or rare things, artfully assembled here, instruct the eye to see and to look" are the words of a French poet, inscribed on the front of a Parisian museum, making the point that we need to train our eyes to see what is true, beautiful, remarkable, authentic, and distinguish it from what is tawdry and sterile even when it is original. Fabrizio has the "eye" and he is able to see. In Bangkok and throughout Thailand, he feeds on art and prowls the palaces, the temples and the museums devouring what he sees like a starving man.

One day he happens to be in the National Museum Bangkok; it's probably his tenth visit, he notices a pavilion, the door of which has been left open, which is as good a reason as any to go in, so he enters. What he finds seems to be a store room, which could be temporary or permanent, he doesn't know, where furniture is piled up, cabinets, chests of all shapes and sizes, made of black lacquered wood, covered with decorative patterns painted in gold. The extraordinary variety of the patterns strikes him immediately. They are not the usual scenes with religious themes – the ones he has seen many times in temples throughout the country. Instead, they are scenes which cannot be construed as mystical metaphors because they represent the everyday, simple life of people going about their ordinary business. Here a man enjoying a cup of tea, there a man enjoying a well-earned siesta in the shadow of a straw hut in his garden, and further off a third pulling on his opium pipe with obvious pleasure.

Fabrizio is all too well aware of the nature of the world of art not to realise that, as soon as they can, as soon as they are freed of political and cultural correctness, artists try to show what they know best, their lives, those of their nearest and dearest, and the world they live in. And without going as far as the probable self-portrait of Michelangelo in the Sistine Chapel in the Vatican, Fabrizio knows that it is the details which are more revealing than the whole.

Amongst the furniture which he discovers, he finds a mammoth piece, a set of four cabinets, each with a double door, each 2.45 m in height, 90 cm in width and designed to be placed in a square formation, one against the other, thus forming a block 2.45 m high and 1.80 m wide, meant to be placed in a space large enough to give access on all sides, so that the entire storage space is usable. But, at the moment, Fabrizio does not have access to all sides because the four units are piled one against the other, and it is only by craning his neck that he can perceive their incredible richness.

This ensemble, which stands on pig-leg-shaped supports, is today used as a manuscript cabinet, to be found in the National Library in Bangkok, on the fourth floor, in a working area with free access, devoted to the study of ancient parchments and rolls; the area offers sufficient space all around to allow one to appreciate every detail. On three of the four elements, there is a depiction of the third grand council of Buddhists, held to revise the Tripitaka, the Buddhist Canon; on the fourth is a scene showing Buddhaghosa, an eminent monk, visiting Sri Lanka, according to the Mahavamsa, the Buddhist literature of Sri Lanka.

What Fabrizio discovers is a bewildering tangle of tiny scenes of daily life, virtually filling the decorated area and leaving only a much-reduced space for the overtly religious elements. The dichotomy between the "religious-institutional" aspect and daily life is further highlighted by the graphic treatment given to them. Everything relating to spiritual traditions is full of rich details, floral, sometimes a little heavy and frequently stiff, whereas the other scenes are executed with simplicity, an austerity which can only be equalled by the "ligne claire" style, the invention of Hergé and the Belgian cartoonists, which made Tintin and other characters worldwide celebrities.

Elsewhere in the same storeroom, so laden with unexpected treasures, is another smaller cabinet decorated with jungle scenes of frolicking birds and animals, which, thanks to Fabrizio, will acquire a world-wide reputation. But for the present it is the photographer who must act. He needs permission to come back and photograph his discoveries.

At the time the National Museum was run by Silpa Bhirasri, who is considered to be the "father" of contemporary Thai art and was born in Italy under the name of Corrado Feroci. He came to Thailand in 1923, at the invitation of the Bangkok government, to assist the country and its artists in setting up their faculty of Fine Arts. Like all Florentines, he was force-fed art from birth, so he personally felt very much at home, whether he was dealing with sculpture, architecture, paintings or the gems of ancient art.

When Fabrizio met Corrado, the two art enthusiasts hit it off immediately. It is easy to imagine how Fabrizio was unsurprisingly impressed by the encyclopaedic

knowledge of the older man and how Corrado was taken with the humanist and sensitive approach of the younger man. Between the two, there develops what the photographer will describe as a "true friendship", a strong relationship in which they meet frequently and discuss endlessly all forms of Thai and Asian art.

Corrado authorises Fabrizio to photograph the lacquer cabinets, but insists that they not be touched or moved. Quite a challenge! But rather than give up the idea which he believes in strongly, Fabrizio agrees. He first makes an electrical extension lead 100 metres long, to the end of which he connects an ordinary 100W light bulb. Then, as the artist explains in his notes, he seeks the assistance of a "friendly hand" to hold the bulb close enough to the details being photographed. Fabrizio takes the photos, and the result is a series of sharply contrasted images which break up the nature of the material being examined to a degree which confuses the eye of the observer: is it a drawing, a painting, an engraving? One has one's doubts but one thing is (falsely) certain, they are not photos!

The photographer has succeeded in overcoming his own material in order to force us to see exactly what the painter dared to represent, these tiny scenes of everyday life of his time and world. The result is fantastic in artistic, cultural and historic terms, like immersing oneself in the society of Siam in days gone by.

Thai painting only uses two surfaces, either wall frescoes in palaces or temples,

Manuscript cabinet, gold decoration on lacquer, late 18th c.
National Museum Bangkok, accession no. 116.

sometimes poorly maintained, or, worse, restored by well-meaning but naive hands; or lacquer panels of furniture or chests serving a variety of purposes. Paradoxically, even today, the painted works which are of immense interest do not particularly attract the attention of art enthusiasts. The reason is simple: these cabinets have been saddled with the description "religious" which seems to dull the aesthetic sense of observers.

So it was that a very distinguished connoisseur of Thai culture to whom these photographs by Fabrizio La Torre were recently shown, made the following comment:

"Yes, it's a religious subject."

"You mean this man, slumped on his veranda drinking tea, is religious?"

After a moment's hesitation:

"Probably a monk..."

"Supposing you are right. You are saying a monk slumped on a veranda, drinking tea is a religious image."

Another momentary silence followed by:

"Well, he may not be completely religious but on the same side of the piece, you do see a religious theme."

"True, but the 'religious theme' only represents no more than 15% of the decoration! The artist takes the opportunity to show lots of other things!"

You can feel the weariness beginning to overcome the connoisseur. So, to put an end to a futile exchange, he finally comes up with an argument which brooks no challenge:

"All this furniture is religious, whatever the decoration, because it was used to store religious texts. Therefore, it is religious."

With that, his patience having reached its limit, the connoisseur turned on his heel, without allowing any opportunity for the last question:

"Is it the structure of Thai society itself which leads to the relative neglect of these brief, naive representations of ordinary people in previous centuries?"

In the history of world art, as taught by Corrado Feroci to his students, the idea that ordinary people can be portrayed alongside the powerful, even in important religious locations, is pretty obvious, even a truism. For example, as a real masterpiece of European medieval art, the stained-glass windows of the cathedral at Chartres, in France, display all the figures of Christianity, the majesty of several kings of that country, but also drapers, coopers, weavers and cobblers of that period. There are many other examples, at least in those religions, such as Buddhism, which allow figurative art.

The technical conditions under which these shots are taken prevent Fabrizio from doing an exhaustive job. Nonetheless, on this huge cabinet in four distinct parts, he captures 21 scenes of everyday life, but is obliged to leave aside 30 or 40 others, all superb and historically valuable, which you can enjoy if you visit the National Museum to see this rarity.

Having returned to Rome and the end of 1961, Fabrizio has these photos enlarged, then fixed on wooden panels. He uses them to decorate his various apartments. For him, these images, in which photography, painting and drawing all come together, are not simply "pictures you have to see" but also doors open to creativity and meditation, pagan symbols giving to each of us a moment of relaxation and inner calm.

The painters who produced these Thai cabinets were first and foremost artists, witnesses to their era, displaying the world with which they were familiar, which was all around them, the world of their wives and their children, their joys and their sadnesses, a human life almost like ours today. By showing us their work, La Torre builds a bridge between these artists and us, so that we can feel the human connection which links us all together.

From the National Museum Bangkok to the Maison Hermès in Paris

Next to the rather non-religious, large cabinet, Fabrizio discovers a somewhat smaller piece of furniture, with decorations from which the human form is completely absent. It is just a jungle, a rather idealised jungle, in which playful squirrels gambol, with good-natured birds, poetic butterflies. A pleasant scene, restful and yet full of energy. In the upper half of the right-hand door, the photographer focusses on a particular spot, which he captures, though slightly receding, given the lack of perspective of the shot. It does not matter to him; he has obtained exactly what he wants, what had caught his attention right from the start.

Scarfs and blouses, Maison Hermès.

As soon as he is back in Rome for a few weeks' holiday, he has the photo printed, enlarged, and fixed on a wooden panel, and then he makes a present of it to his mother Gabriella, aged 70 at the time, but who is still an active artist, painting on porcelain and inventing scarf patterns for Maison Hermès.

Fabrizio is careful not to tell his mother what he had in mind when photographing this detail. He smiles and says nothing, waiting for Gabriella's inevitable question, asking him if, one day, this pretty jungle scene might, in his opinion, be transformed into a silk scarf for the renowned Maison Hermès.

And that day came around, to the amusement of mother and son who realise that without a doubt, in this family, the most generally shared trait is the artist's eye! Gabriella La Torre produced her design and entrusted it to her friend Jean Guerrand, one of the executives of the Maison Hermès, who decided to produce the scarf in various colours and to use the design in sportswear items (tops, sweaters, blousons, etc.).

Unfortunately, somewhere along the production line of this scarf, someone not well acquainted with Asian art decides to call it "Old China" and overlook its Thai origin. This is something of a blunder, which is all the more surprising since Hermès is justly proud of having been chosen at the beginning of the 20th century to supply a number of prestigious deliveries to the Royal Court of the King of Siam, and in 1905 to supply the harnesses for the horse-drawn vehicle of the Siamese ambassador in Paris. Perhaps one day this "Old China" will become the "Old Siam" it always should have been, particularly since this peaceful jungle pattern, nowadays frequently chosen to illustrate real Thai art, is rapidly acquiring the status of a modern icon.

The photos taken by Fabrizio La Torre in the National Museum are an invitation particularly addressed to young Thais but also to enthusiasts the world over, to take back these scenes from everyday life and these decorative motifs which, in their gaiety, their abundance and their diversity, are offered to us to enhance our lives. Two art-loving Italians, Corrado Feroci and Fabrizio La Torre, saw before us all the creative energy to be drawn from these panels. Let us follow in their footsteps: the beautiful, the joyful and the authentic remain vital to happiness.

ACKNOWLEDGEMENTS

Since the re-opening of the photographic archives of Fabrizio La Torre in 2009, a small group, composed of accomplished specialists in the indispensable areas of technical expertise in addition to a number of others who were simply enthusiastic about such a great adventure, who have all become close, indispensable friends, has taken on the job of presenting this remarkable body of work and highlighting the engaging character of the artist.

First and foremost, Jean-Pierre De Neef, a brilliant printer of art photos, who took on the daunting task of restoring negatives and digitising photographs, working from the outset with the artist, thus learning to understand his tastes and wishes.

Yves Kengen, a Dutch journalist in Brussels, who has supplied essential assistance both with respect to this book and to the whole of the Bangkok operation, even coming several times to the Thai capital to check on progress. At his side, Pierre Swennen, a Belgian citizen, a long-time resident in Thailand, who acted as a gifted and charming "fixer" as well as a local correspondent.

As all the original documents for this book were either in French or Italian, Patrizia Vaccani and Peter Corrigan were the highly competent translators, responsible for this English version.

A late addition to the team, but who quickly made herself indispensable thanks to her encyclopaedic knowledge of Thai art and history, the academic Dominique Le Bas knows how much we owe her.

A word of thanks to Florence Rodriguez, who conducted a number of conversations with the artist before his death which have contributed to this book. Discovering with us some reels of 16 mm film shot in Bangkok by Fabrizio La Torre, Marie Iannucci, as a consummate professional, immediately realised their quality.

Next, Lila Van der Meulen, who seems to have mastered almost all of the cinematic arts, succeeded in editing the remarkable films which visitors to the Bangkok exhibitions will be able to enjoy.

In Brussels, having worked for more than a year on this project, young Louise Audouin has been the painstaking archivist and documentalist of which we were in dire need.

All the persons mentioned know they have contributed to making the works of their friend Fabrizio La Torre better known, via a non-profit-making body which survives thanks to the contributions it receives. Thus, their work constitutes an act of commitment, benevolence and generosity. They are owed an enormous vote of thanks.

Since the protection of culture is an enthralling struggle which is often bereft of financial means, let us also offer our thanks to those persons, who, in the name of their friendship for the artist or simply to support an unexpected and original project, gave that financial assistance without which nothing is possible, Rita Nisi, Martine Tessari, Susanna Bologna and Jean-Pierre Laffont.

And then we have all those who have been part of this adventure since the beginning, the moment when we opened to the public those archives which had been hidden for so long, when the artist at the end of his life finally received the recognition which was overdue and when constant support, friendship and encouragement from all were indispensable: Christine Bayle and her husband Marco Benedetti always at our side offering encouragement and solidarity to Fabrizio and the team of Brussels Art Edition; Ambassador Tran Van Thinh and Brigitte Loustau taking the art of hospitality to new levels; Giovanni Caracciolo di Vietri and Robert Alfonsi who made the artist's first encounter with his public possible and afterwards proffering good advice; finally, with great patience and offering a helping hand when needed, Jules Bayle and Serena de Chabot, who played an important and innovative role in relation to another book devoted to Fabrizio La Torre.

Close to Fabrizio, accompanying him in opening his art to the public, his family members Pierre Bayle and Béatrice Bayle-Ghiliotti demonstrated their affection for the man and the artist.

Finally, in the rather unusual story of this artist and the belated revelation of his work, a particular tribute should be paid to HSH Prince Albert II of Monaco, who, by deciding to host the first La Torre Retrospective in 2014, allowed the artist to devote every minute of the last year of his life to tireless labour on his archives. Without that work, this book would not have been possible: we would never have discovered Fabrizio La Torre's view of Thailand and Asia. A warm vote of thanks to the Prince and all the members of the team at the Cultural Affairs Department of Monaco.

Having been one of the first Thais to see the photos taken in Bangkok by Fabrizio, Shane Suvikapakornkul agrees to be the publisher of this work, and is aware of the esteem and friendship in which we hold him.

Thank you all for your help and support. Nothing is more thrilling than taking part in the flowering of artistic expression: the photos of Fabrizio La Torre collected here are a proof of how worthwhile were the efforts made to show them to a wider public.

ISBN 978-1-932476-91-0

Published in 2018 by
Serindia Publications, Inc.
Chicago, Illinois, USA
info@serindia.com
www.serindia.com

Design and Layout: Serindia Studio

Printed in China

Cataloging-in-Publication Data of this volume is available from the Library of Congress.